# Iridescent

## Salina Trahan

" Exposing luminous true colors displayed from different perspectives "

**Iridescent**

©Salina Trahan, 2020

ISBN: 978-0-578-70147-9

i

This book is for the person who feels lost.
This book is for the person recovering from rock bottom.
This book is for the person who has been burned by love.
This book is for the person who hasn't realized they lost faith.
This book is for a person who is in a period of transformation.
This book is for the person who will make it through.

# Table Of Contents

## Reflection

## Ownership

# Foreword

This book is dedicated to the playlist of emotions felt while spiraling with no awareness on where to go or how you even ended up in this space.

When being hurt can no longer be ignored, you must acknowledge the cause of such pain to find freedom from the discomfort. Everyone has their own journey and process to go through rather than to get over. If you are to get caught in a comfort zone beware, it can kill. The comfort zone is a distraction limiting your ablity to find hope for your greatest desires.

You have buried toxic things in your heart that have now tampered and darkened your spirit.

It is now time to acknowledge it, feel it, and own it.

That is where you will find the ability to leverage the pieces of vulnerability that have been hidden away. That is the space to truly be open minded to take ownership over the matters regarding your heart.

This is the sweet spot where  the reactions of others based on your life experiences no longer hold influence.

This is where confidence grows knowing you are not stagnate in the stew of your mistakes.

Progression is key but very few talk about those grey areas that changed their lives forever. This was my period of distress that I made it through. I continue to move forward transparently, treasuring this perfectly crafted rock bottom iridescently.

x

# Iridescent Stages to Healing

| | |
|---|---|
| **Free Flow** | Remember the positives that opened the door to love that person, situation, or environment. |
| **Transparency** | Be real. Be upfront . You may even still have hope alive. Here is a free space to put it all on the table. |
| **Through** | Explore your anger, denial, or even depression. It's ok to feel it all, only to grow stronger and make it through. |
| **Acceptance** | The reality has always been there awaiting to be acknowledged. |
| **Reflection** | There is meaning through every encounter that impacts your heart. Remember those critical moments that created lasting impact. |
| **Ownership** | Commit to becoming the person you will become from iridescent healing . |

# Freely flow to begin healing

Have your heart and mind ready to connect.
Ready to be vulnerable.
Ready to be understood and prepared to forgive.
This captured journey to healing is not a linear nor sequential experience.
This book is not a politically correct declaration.
Instead, this is a book full of raw reflections, transparent thoughts, and fragile feelings. These elements display the aftermath of love being weaponized.
To ignite the healing process, one must grieve the layers shed, allowing space for the heart to breathe again.
It's the little things that can accumulate in your heart and manifest an emotional rock bottom. A rock bottom so low, it taught you things the mountain tops could never display.

*"It was this book that provided the true closure I not only wanted but needed to let my iridescent light shine from within."*

I am flourishing in the grey areas...

# Free Flow

Heart-wrenching traumas seemingly start with lucid thoughts and effortless bliss. That bliss is filled with love, memories, and comfort while still leaving room for fear to foster.
A bliss that reckless.
A bliss that clouds judgment.
A bliss that has yet to be experienced until now.
This bliss provides an endless supply of liberating happiness.
This undeniable happiness is paired with unforgettable memories divinely crafted by two beautiful souls.
As they freely live in comfort and embrace every pillar building their free-flowing love. They pray this freely flowing bliss is a limitless supply, flourishing as it continuously feeds their spirits. Unfortunately, the end is closer than expected, with only one half to this whole fully aware.

**Author Reflection:**

*Imagine a love so powerful being the pull to a bow, ready to fire a shock wave to your soul. Yet, you are unaware of the angle at which such a blow would penetrate your heart. I wonder how you would handle the transparency of those luminous true colors you never knew existed.*

It's honestly such a beautiful deception seen glistening through the tears shed in solitude. This journey was ignited from having my heart broken by a laundry list of red flags and warning signals overlooked. These toxic love lessons have been suppressed for years. No soul owner caused this deeply rooted vulnerability.
It came from family, friends, situation-ships, my career, and most of all myself. At some point in my journey, I knew I wanted to heal from these traumas and ultimately grow stronger from those negatives. The start of my process flowed from remembering the good times, the carefree moments, and the pure love that exuded. Remembering these positives helped me to relinquish the fear of loving again, trusting others, and growing healthy relationships all around. In this process, I refilled a hole in my heart with this newfound liberation and self-love.
Pure self-respect and worth.
This process reminded me how beautiful and good it feels to fall in love with myself so freely. It uplifted my soul to learn the power love possesses through it all. This ever-evolving journey is the yin to follow up the yang of my darkest period of growth. This journey is hardly perfect and

*is full of ups and downs. It is full of honesty broadcasted from the heart while navigating through a grey area love, life, and relationships caused. This journey showcases two different points of view to capture all that was felt in moments of reflection. So, sit back and get ready for a ride. I hope it opens your heart to reflect the truth, the experiences, and the love that has created an impact in your life. We all face our own personal rock bottoms that very few will ever know. Allow my vulnerability to spark an outpour of transparency, acceptance, reflection, and ownership to help lead you to a safe space to heal.*

# Hide & Seek

One single exchange of honesty can ignite such a
euphoric shift in one's spirit. As the two of you
start to explore the identity of each other, this flirtatious
feeling multiplies and feels vaguely familiar. The potential
of what could be is immensely overstimulating to your
heart. With each beat unfolding a portrait of unity, family,
and sustainability. This scorching sensation circulates with
every beat of your heart. Racing rapidly as your body tries
to reject these feelings.
The rejection is orchestrated out of fear.
The fear of being hurt.
The fear of being used.
The fear of being cheated on.
The fear of being ghosted.
This rapid circulation of negativity is placed on a
generation left not knowing how to really love. The fear is
a protection mechanism but something about this person
eliminates it all. By sharing these vulnerabilities, it creates
open space for love to live and thrive. Simply craving to
know what's beyond the surface level. To know what has
constructed this individual's characteristics and
experiences.

With each passing day one question alone starts to dwell...
are they the one?
The one who has cracked open a piece of that radiant heart. The one exposing the raw feelings of unexpected iridescent love.
It's the domino effect allowing each of your spirit's to coil as one. It's that burning desire to be wanted, loved, and accepted unconditionally.
But is that real or is it the idea of happily ever after hiding in their subconscious?
It's a hopeless romantic high resembling love that never truly hits the same. As time passes, the feeling of being stuck lingers. This twinkling love cuts deep. As it has burrowed itself in your heart waiting as if you are playing hide and seek.

# The Little Things

The love for all the little things.
The subtle reminders.
The love for the intricacies that make us unique.
Those little things construct a foundation to love a variety of individuals. Each leaves traces of love lessons ingrained and triggered when someone tries to find their way to your heart. Their transparency can reflect a radiant love perched on the walls creating a barrier around your heart. They leverage those things as proof of paying attention to the little details that speak to your heart.
It's the little things that construct the foundation and patterns of a relationship.
It's the little things that flash before you when it's all over.
It's also the little things that get dismissed when you think you have fallen in love.
It's the bits of sacrifices made simply in the name of love.

**Author Reflection:**
*The little things that caught me were the surprises that put a smile on my face daily. The intuitive gestures made me feel wanted and included in that particular someone's world. Just like in the movies, those little goodbye kisses left me thinking about that person all day long. We shared the vulnerable truths to our past*

*and the losses that followed. This person selflessly blessed me with the things I loved knowing they would never indulge. I had been celebrated in such small ways, yet realizing how much they cared was truly valued. I appreciated our escape into the treetops even though deep down, I am scared of heights. But it was those highs that lifted my spirit. We found peace in nature, looking out to see the bright possibilities of the future. This collaboration was a blissful necessity in that moment of our lives. So exceptionally balanced, knowing our spirits had intertwined in such a short period. Those little things are the small attachments that infiltrate my mind and slide through the cracks of my prophetic dreams. Those are the little things that make it hard just to let it be.*

# Your Sweet Nothings

Ever sat and daydreamed...
wondering what was on that person's mind before the
storm hit? What possible sweet things would that
certain someone say knowing their actions in the
near future? All of that exuded effort, those sweet
gestures would no longer hold value.
Welp, it would probably go something like this:
This time has by far been one to remember.
From nothing to something, literally. You are a
fantastic being, soul, and energy. I am fortunate to
know you in this light. You are meant for GREAT
THINGS, and I will do everything in my power to help.
You came into my life exactly when I needed a friend,
and you've become so much more.
I love you!
As a FRIEND, always.
As a woman genuinely.
As mine, eventually.
I will always be here—a call, text, facetime, a flight
away. I love you with my entire heart.
I'm in love with you.
Thank you for being here.
I appreciate you more than you know.
Love always,

_____

**Author Reflection:**

*You filled a blank space that remained empty for years. No one has ever been able to fill my heart as you did. We shared so much in this space and time. We created a bond of our own. A bond Lord only knows the depths too. This bond of trust, love, and memories. I want you to know that you mattered to me.*

# Transparency

Would you be able to handle the transparency of blindingly luminous true colors you never knew existed?

It's easily the just bitter truth.

Reality is here smacking you in the head, causing deep-rooted confusion. It has you questioning how could something so "perfect" be crushingly toxic? The master plan was mapped out, but my how things shift when life hits. What is one supposed to do? There is no such thing as quitting, so chin up and stay in the fight.

Do it.

Even if it scares you.

Even if you have to toss your pride to the side.

Even if you feel like you have already failed.

Even if embarrassment is lurking in your subconscious.

BE TRANSPARENT ABOUT HOW YOU FEEL!

# Seven Days

Intuition is a difficult skill to manipulate for your benefit.
It starts as a feeling in your gut. It proceeds to manifest in your
mind, but the love inhibits your ability to leverage your intuition,
sending warning signals to your heart.
Be careful because the switch-up is real.
You're lost, not knowing what's going on, and it feels like you're
losing them in seven days.
Seven is the number of completeness and perfection. Yet the
feelings your heart lack the essence of seven. Emotions are
shaken up, feeling chilled and on the rocks. Your mind is
swirling around thoughts of doubt, weakness, and second-
guessing. Slowly lingering is that feeling of being alone and
being isolated. Like clockwork, darkness clouds your judgment.
Blocking out every bit of joy in its path, trying to murder any
ideas of hope as if you did not deserve them. This was the
perfectly crafted cocktail for you to feel disconnected
internally... spiritually. It's consuming your mind, and alternative
feelings begin to surface through this moment of distress.
Feelings that did not embody the desires in your heart and soul.
This was dark; you never wanted to come back to life. This was
the call for help to admit finally...
"I don't think I am okay."
Well, it turns out this was the vulnerable truth you chose to
leave them out of. You so quickly feeling the need to create
your sustainability and strength to uphold your half of this

relationship.

Unfortunately, you feel them pulling back.

You feel them being distant.

You feel them shifting without a mention of what's going through their mind.

So overwhelmed, not knowing what to do. You start constructing permanent solutions, manifested out of a temporary mindset lost in a sea of confusion. Your genuine doubts scared them. Even though, deep down, it was not all entirely true.

If you do not fix something or make changes within yourself, this concept of a year will soon be obsolete. This pivotal year was used as an indicator to be united and accomplished. This year to get our shit together. This year too... this year for what?

Behind doubt and misery lies action and determination. This is the fuel to help push through every time.

They were never damaging to your week until this point when everything around you felt like it was falling apart.

At this time...

THIS critical and cruel moment of weakness they muted the aura and energy that had connected the two of you.

The person you wanted to talk to was gone.

The person you became attached to was gone.

The person you kept at the forefront of what mattered pulled away like the last string to tread, holding the rope together.

Shutting out all lines of communication. Thus, enticing

your wandering mind and sending your heart into an uproar. The command center of your emotions is erupting and getting ready to implode.

All you want is to be in a permanent happy place.

A safe and blissful space.

All hope is clinging on to that last piece of thread. As if you're on a tightrope, holding your breath, waiting to see if they will be there to catch you. It had seemed like you regrouped a solid foundation for everything, making the past four seven days hell. But now, your present seven days are incomplete.

**Author Reflection:**
*I thought I had fixed everything except for the person at the core of my heart. I made all these changes without asking what their needs were as the other half to my whole. They were so strong, but I'm supposed to be there with them every step of the way. I pray it's not too late.*
*I hope I didn't destroy us in seven days.*

# Sign. Sealed. Undelivered

*Friend or … If I say I will love you and support you through the good and the bad, I will always stay true to that.*
*I hate being disconnected from you.*
*It's like a blackout in the city of emotions living in my heart once energized by your endless supply of I love you's.*
*It was true simplicity.*
*Our time spent was one for the books.*
*Clearly, this book...*
*full of stories about this journey to recovery.*
*It was the raw recklessness with lack of protection over my heart that led me here. It hurts, and it didn't have to be this way. Thinking about walking up to your beautiful face every day was the best feeling in the world. Playing in your hair, glancing at your baby freckles, and at last, glaring into your golden-brown eyes. You greeted my ears with a compelling I love you taking my breath away, making it nearly impossible to say it back at times.*
*Not sure if it was the shock that our feelings were mutual or the little voice in my head saying run, it's too good to be true.*
*Either way, it melted my heart, overpowering the doubts.*
*With time, I knew my love for you had grown deeply consuming my heart, mind, and soul.*
*Our talks gave me insight, in between long kisses until the sun kissed the night. That very moment would remind us of yet another*

*day that had gone by. That day turned into weeks. Those weeks turned into months. Those months turned into ...*
*To think,*
*this all started with gentle touches and subtle exchanges of affectionate energy. Your alluring glare, paired with that smile, heated my soul. Finding out the potential of this could increase my apprehension as I knew there was a chance that I would fall in love with you.*
*I guess one could say my greatest fear came true because of you. Falling asleep in your arms night after night. Finding my perfect fit lying next to you. It just worked.*
*We worked.*
*You were easy.*
*You were my bliss.*
*You were my joy.*
*The way you pulled me in closer to you made me feel so safe. You so easily navigated through my emotions and painted such a beautiful portrait of our future.*
*Yes, I can go on and on because these are just a few things that made me fall in love... These are the happy thoughts. Thoughts that remind me of how captivating love could be. It would be easier if these feelings would go away as quickly as you did out of my life, mind, presence, and heart. I am here regardless. I love you. Keep thinking about your hopes, dreams, and greatest desires.*

# Paint & Sip

*Why is this anxious feeling derived from thoughts of you?
I'm trying to put positivity out while simultaneously trying to
find distractions to fill this void. Painting is the only tedious
thing that can distract me from this internal hole
constructed from heartbreak and emotional imbalance.
This wine is the true medicine to relax every ounce
of my existence.
My heart...
it feels like the entire bottom half shut down. It was once
so easy to visualize the look in your eyes when you said I
meant everything to you... from the bottom of your heart.
It's pretty ironic.
This poetic declaration was bullshit.
I should have known then. I should have taken my time,
like steady strokes on a canvas, to ease my mind.
It seems like I've cried more than I have in my entire
lifetime. I can't stop thinking about you. Knowing there is a
chance I will never get back what we had.
You just quit.
You just gave upon us.
As if you had been waiting to do this for some time but just
hadn't found the right ditch. I was shocked at first, naïve to
think it was me or something I could fix. But today, I am
just anxious, feeling like I'm due for a breakdown at the
moment. Lord, please allow me*

*the energy to be happy, financially stable, and loved unconditionally.*
*Today I saw a butterfly.*
*What is the meaning of this?*
*Yesterday it poured.*
*Just like it was pouring rain when driving to get here.*
*Pouring like me refiling my glass and letting my emotions spill all over this canvas.*

# Limbo

*I have opened up.*
*I have finally poured my heart out.*
*At least part of it.*
*For the first time, I fought for what made me feel so vulnerable. I tried not once, not twice, but several times and then some. I have admitted my errors. I have been willing and wanting to talk, but you have built this invisible wall between us, waiting to place the final brick in place. I can't help but feel like my soul is in a state of limbo, shocked by your actions. I have been relentless, yet you still choose to strip yourself of even the slightest residue of my existence. You say your past downfalls resulted in the inability to follow your intuition, enabling you to jump ship and leave me deserted.*
*It's as if I had lost my value.*
*No longer treasured.*
*Yes, I had doubts, but it was rooted in no action being taken to correct my imbalance. The imbalance of being shaken by shifts in tides crashing into my world. The imbalance of supports is missing to keep my spirit uplifted. We made it through the waves of your issues. Yet sank when mine appeared like an iceberg in the sea of my reality. You pulled back so quickly without any hesitation. I can't help but question... how valid were those confessions of love to you?*

*Every time, my strides to reach out are left pending.*
*I have a single shred of hope left, but it's as if a tight grip*
*has been clamped around the valves to my heart. Limiting*
*the circulation of hope, thus putting my mind in a state of*
*limbo.*

# Through

The growing pains of life are best experienced when you go through the pain and feel it all. Once you come out from the other side, there stands this refined version of yourself.

# Heart In Hibernation

*My heart has fallen asleep.*
*I can't say I am heartbroken because I can't feel*
*anything at this point. It's as if my heart has been*
*marinated in liquor, steady trying to duplicate the*
*warm and fuzzy stimulation you once did. My heart*
*is trying so hard to reset, but my mind keeps*
*creating instant replays of our short-lived fantasy.*
*I guess it's true; our connection is dead.*
*Those blasts of our past are all that races through*
*my mind when I try to sleep. I'm steady taking sips*
*of wine to silence this discomfort.*
*My most genuine aspiration is to fall in love, but it*
*seems that the entire narrative is a hoax.*
*Time and time again, I open up, only to be left*
*continuously crushed—every time I hold a little more*
*back, and it seems never to be enough.*
*Where do I go from here?*
*Will I ever find the one, or is it a settling game?*
*What am I willing to look the other way for?*
*This enables the compromise of my own*
*comfortably. Yet serves as a quick fix for temporary*
*comfort found in others.*
*I want to cry, but I don't think there are any more*
*tears left. God bless this pink Moscato sending my*
*heart into hibernation.*

# Road Trip

*I am a young twenty-something year old.*
*I just moved across the county to mark my declaration of*
*independence. Before this certain someone, I had plans*
*and a clear view of where I was going. I was good without*
*them. I constantly question why God placed them in the*
*middle of my path like a captivating sight to see. I wanted*
*to ride, never imagining the wheels would fall off. Now I am*
*lost, off road trying to handle the loss of you.*
*Not knowing where to go from here.*
*I can talk and develop a great exit strategy for the stand-*
*still God has put me in. But that's it,*
*God has made it clear.*
*In this space and time, God is telling me, forcing me to*
*have several seats. Until this point, I have been on the*
*move, wound up so tight with this tunnel vision of a plan to*
*pursue my ultimate happiness.*
*But what is my ultimate happiness?*
*What will make me happy?*
*Who will make me happy?*
*I fell in love and let this person in.*
*The moment I showed doubt, emotional weakness, and*
*raw vulnerability they were gone.*

At the end of the day, they had several issues on the surface level and were probably not the top pick of my mother's approval.

Despite it all, what caught me on their web was the way they treated me.

The way they included me.

The way they embraced some flaws I haven't even accepted.

They were there for me.

They were always available.

Just a phone call away.

They loved me.

They appreciated my craving to be united, peaceful, and live so happily. They peered into the windows of my soul, filling me up with all the things I hoped to hear from the love of my life. It was as if they craved having control of my heart. Knowing I would be blinded.

I didn't ask for this, and as I recall, this person planted the seed. This person who so openly and candidly craved for this to happen.

"You're going to fall in love with me" rolled off their tongue, plaguing my garden of hopes and desires. I wish I would have known how committed this person would be. To nurture that seed, strictly for simple pleasure. When I commit and solidify that spot for someone in my heart, I am with them no matter what. I need someone who will stick by me in the long run. To share this open road of life. I'm not the type to hop from one situation to the next. And *to think, the person crying in my arms claiming to have abandonment issues orchestrated a perfect recipe for me to feel the residue of pain left from their past traumas.*

*This time it's not me but you.*

*You are the engineer of your own unhappiness, and you were so close to breaking my spirit. Our love was an unforgettable journey. You were showing flashes of your true character on that short and bitter-sweet road trip.*

# Happy :Our

*I have a few gulps of wine after a long day.*
*Mm-hmm, our memories still bring me to tears.*
*I wake up feeling like my spirit is misplaced in this*
*body of mine. Every day, I open my eyes,*
*overwhelmed, my heart racing, and unable to take a*
*deep breath.*
*I'm not calm, but I am at ease for what seems like*
*only an minute at this daily happy hour.*
*This hour starts when the sun rises, numbing me to*
*ensure a blissful fall to get through the night.*
*Everything is an experience and a learning lesson,*
*they say. The good and the bad. I have to be*
*confident in what I feel, think, and want. I have to be*
*unapologetically vulnerable and not allow the*
*reaction of others to hold me back.*
*This is my life.*
*This is my happiness.*
*I am twenty-something with a whole lot more life to*
*live. Love is not supposed to be a half of*
*indulgence. But when it is... just*
*don't let it creep up inside of your soul.*
*Cheers to a tremendous Happy :Our.*

# Double Edge Sward

The home-cooked meals. The foot rubs. The
intellectual stimulation. The hold me close and
never let go moments...
All were exuded to keep you distracted from the
truth. That special someone broadcasted their
intentions as clear as day. Yet on multiple
occasions, you chose to dismiss everything related
to your "high standards" and accepted the bare
basics. Those warning signals were displayed time
and time again. But the salesman always had the
perfect pitch ready to discredit those concerns.
Broken spirits have a hard time planting themselves
in a garden full of pure love, trust, patience, and
understanding. So unable to receive the nutrients
that will get them through the drought of their
current life pitfalls.
Feeling so safe in one's hands, but in an uttered
breath of transparency, you are told you mean
nothing to them. Their actions had proven the
choice made in their heart long before you arrived.
So optimistic and unwilling to accept the truth from
the very beginning. You are now caught up in
emotions and

tender massages easing your wondering mind. It incarcerates the intuition locked away, trying not to die. Only to leave you vulnerable, wishing you had acted on those gut-wrenching senses inside.

**Author Reflection:**
*You are; you were my double edge sward. The big strong man before me was constructed by trauma, mommy issues, and self-manifested stagnation. So stuck in a dream, having such a false sense of what a sustainable reality is. So unable to adapt, cope, and progress forward.*
*Simply content with life passing you by.*
*So unwilling to wake up and have some drive. A burning desire to make moves right here and now. Strategic moves that will generate stability for the future. So unable to manifest the beautiful wants and desires we talked about time and time again. To break the cycle of broken households and toxic marriages.*
*To indeed be happy and in love.*
*Your warmth, your comfort, your presence, and your physical touch are what kept you in the spin cycle of my reality. Replicating love like actions I desperately wanted to cling to.*
*But why? For what?*

*Why did you keep me knowing my heart?*
*Knowing my intentions?*
*Knowing the type of love I bring to the table?*
*Why didn't you let me go knowing this was not what you wanted?*
*It just sucks. And to top it off, the person who is supposed to show me how a man is to treat a woman.*
*To respect a woman.*
*To love a woman.*
*To protect a woman.*
*To encourage a woman.*
*To champion the queen they selected to stand by their side.*
*My father.... replicated the exact behaviors of my double edge sward. We aren't perfect, but I wonder if the double edge swards of the world ever think about their actions' being a ripple effect?*
*This hopeless romantic thing is such a double edge sword.*
*Dammed if you do. Dammed if you don't.*
*How is one ever to learn how to love when the toxicity dilutes the levels of love left remaining in your heart?*

# Acceptance

The dust has settled and
you partially have all the facts. You are feeling
stressed, anxious, and lost. Unfortunately, the cause
of this overwhelming sense is stemming from one
crucial thing. Your brewing stress is equally
connected to your inability to accept the reality of
what you have gone through. My dear, you are
someone that is struggling to cope. That is the area of
focus for you to gain humbling acceptance.

**Author Reflection:**

*Acceptance comes in many ways and forms. My
acceptance glistened from the clarity uniquely crafted from
past experiences. They are grey areas that helped me
transition into a space of healing and reflection.*

# Great Escape

*Dear God, Thank you for giving me life! I am so far from perfect but wear the mask as if I am. I am so sick of the mask. So unable to identify or even tap into my real emotions. My mask is cracking away, and piece by piece, there is a beautiful lotus thriving underneath, waiting to burst through the darkness the mask brings. We don't all want to wear the mask. We want to be free from the mask.*

*The mask.*

*The mask.*

*The mask, oh thee, but do we want to be free? It has been there to hide our harsh cries.*

*There to be a deceitful lie of happiness that is truly filled with the great depression of my spirit.*

*The feeling of emptiness and being alone is constantly dwelling. I'm feeling isolated, not knowing how to shake this feeling. Waiting for an answer but so shut down, I can't even hear it.*

*But once the mask is on, there is no being alone. It's the mask, the mask and me, the mask and I, the mask to we.*

*Split perfectly.*

*50/50*

*Do we want to be free of the mask ... Or is the mask our true escape?*

# Poor Connect

It's one thing to feel the loss of someone deep down inside, but how do you cope with the loss of someone who still exists?

The person you care about is out of reach, and the poor connection has not been resolved. You yet again are stuck with a box of memorabilia as proof of their existence once in your presence. Imagine having to pass their exit to reach most destinations every day. Yet, the X on your map is marked with their name as your safe place. You love them, and somehow that is not enough. You want to be embraced with their warmth and circulating blissful energy as you lay your head on their chest. As you lay there, feeling the vibrations of their heart pulsating. The two of your hearts are rhythmically in sync. Anxiously knowing soon you'll have to let go.

This moment right here is all you need.

All you have wanted.

All you have been craving.

As the two of you peer into each other's eyes, knowing this feeling is uniquely crafted by your shared cadence. As you think to yourself, "I love you so deeply. It's a forever kind of thing." The static noise has muffled these words meant strictly for your soul.

I guess it's time to accept that your connection is poor…

Indefinitely.

# Deep Breaths

*Today felt like a day where I started to breathe again. You constantly took my breath away but little did I know you were capable of consuming it all. You were sucking all the energy and light that filled my spirit. I must have just been a fun plaything to you.*
*A cute little challenge you've had your eye on for a while.*
*A challenge you questioned, wondering if it could be conquered.*
*Congratulations!!*
*\*round of applause\**
*You played yourself.*
*So eager to play like you had it all together.*
*You were telling each one of us a different scene that cast you as the victim. You had the master plan for the most incredible plot twist of my life. You played your part so well, only to hide the truths about what truly holds you back in life. I now see why you are in a repetitive pattern of*
*"Life is always knocking me down."*
*"When it rains, it pours."*
*"I always get the short end of the stick."*
*How do you ever expect the trajectory of your life to dramatically shift when you lack the strength to step outside the comfort zone of what already exists. Not realizing it's the comfort that silently kills.*
*You stick with what's familiar.*

*Such a stagnant level of taste.*
*It's honestly pitiful to see someone with so much*
*potential never switch up the pace.*
*You choose comfortability overgrowth.*
*I will be much further than you down the line, as you*
*are mounted to the time capsule of your mistakes.*
*Never learning the lessons; instead, try to finesse the*
*hell out of them. You try to get around situations only to*
*prolong your struggle. You invested energy into*
*temporary gratifications, leaving behind a trail of*
*negative memories and broken hearts. If you genuinely*
*want to get somewhere, you have to stop trying to skip*
*the struggle. That is where character is built.*
*Embrace it, learn from it, grow from it.*
*But Fuck It. Fuck y— you get the point. I can't afford to*
*care anymore. But It seems like my heart isn't giving*
*me a choice.*
*Crippling my ability to let go.*
*Deep breaths in and out going so slow.*

# Grey

Life does not always go as planned, and sometimes
you get stuck in a delicate grey area.
You have no idea what's to come.
You have no idea what options will be put on the table.
This grey area is a place you have never been before.
It's starting to affect you to the core.
You are waiting and hoping for the sunshine to
breakthrough, pleading with God to follow through.
Unknown.
Simply not knowing what to do.
All you can do is find small bright spots to submerge
those grey areas in.
This is your journey, your rough patch.
Right now, I am flourishing in the grey area and
searching for my inner light, love, and happiness.

# Reflection

Are your eyes wide open now?
Is your heart raw from the pain?
Congratulations, you are well on your way to developing a new level of strength. The reality of the situation is that you cannot control the actions of others. In that mindset, you cannot allow a person, environment, or situation to overwhelm your spirit and create imbalance. You are unique, and God has placed untouchable gifts inside of you that can never be stripped away. Be grateful for this moment of reflection. This is the building block to the foundation of your transformation.

# Jumping

*I am searching for my next come-up to get me out of this hole of distress. But how am I supposed to put my best foot forward when mentally I am at my lowest point.*
*I feel like a failure.*
*I feel like I've messed everything up.*
*I am scared.*
*What if this was the one life-changing decision that permanently screwed up the future of my life?*
*I have no idea what I want.*
*I have no idea where to go.*
*I have no idea how to get over this.*
*I have dug a hole for myself and can't even see the top surrounded in this darkness. I am scared, and very few have a clear idea. I can't ask for help because then, and only then, the ownership of my reality is honestly an embarrassment.*
*I don't have it together.*
*As an adult, the worst feeling in the world is when you can't take care of yourself in this world.*
*Who knew life had such a steep price?*
*But I've already jumped, waiting for the pressure of gravity to*
*let*
*me*
*go.*

# Adulting News Flash

*I am gradually finding peace, balance, and acceptance. I think about my past love lessons sporadically. I remind myself that I will rise, I will be ok, I am strong. I've been trying to revamp my ideas for my next career move. I have never really thought about this due to the strong influence and foundation laid by my mother.*
*Welp, here is what to consider:*

*Can I see myself doing this for 30 years?*

*Can the salary cover living expenses, car notes, cell phone, gas, insurance, savings, travel, pay off debt, etc.?*

*What benefits do they have?*
*You WILL NOT be young forevvaaaa.*

*What are the work hours?*
*NAMASTE balanced between work and life.*
*Am I doing something that connects or supports my passions?*

*You'll need this to stay motivated through the highs and the majority of the lows.*

*It's important to know yourself in regards to your worth and your happiness. Life, relationships, and work will never be stress-free. There will always be a set of challenges to handle. Acknowledging that you you worth it; will ensure your ability to regulate in those relentlessly tough a\*\* spots. They will pop up, and it will seem like the end of the world, but it's always temporary. Continue to explore what makes you happy when you are alone. That is the remedy to gain inner strength.*
*Extra! Extra! Read all about it!*
*Here's your adulting News Flash.*

# Warning Signals

*A first kiss, like a scene out of a movie that I've
seen replay time and time again. Yet, when it
became my reality, it made my heart stop.
It filled my body with this unexplored energy.
I felt it spreading all over, and nothing could put
these feelings to a halt.
That damn kiss made my heart flutter, plastering a
smile so bright, competing with the beauty of the
sunset. That moment felt so complete.
This was new.
This was so compellingly unexpected.
It was the start of something dangerous.
We spent our first night together tossing and
turning in different positions...
Simply just talking.
Listening to the thoughts and scripts of our
lives. In that space, it seemed like a hole had
punctured the ocean of your past. It was like a
flood of thoughts and snapshots of your life being
vocalized.
It was your release.
I listened.
Not taking a stance.
Not giving advice but simply just listening.
I was so captivated to know more I wanted more.
To be embraced by your existence, surrounded by*

your love and covered in your warm hugs and kisses.
For the first time in my life, it was impossible to hold back. There was no overthinking when you were in my presence. I couldn't let go knowing this was something so far left. I let you in but never did I think months later that moment... these thoughts... would be all that was left. So quickly, I fell for you, and step by step, you assured me the feelings were mutual. You said you would send innuendos. Lord knows I had no idea what they were when you first said it.
But it came full circle.
It was those innuendos I missed that could have given me the warning signals.
Signals to guard my heart, protect my energy, my mind, and stabilize my serenity. In that full circle, you became so many things to me.
My soundboard to share my inner thoughts.
My open book, who knows all the things I try to hide. I loved everything that you were to me at that moment. But it's becoming clear that you for me in that moment was always written to be temporary.
I wonder if you ever felt inadequate to be with someone like me?
I wonder if you ever thought about what we could have been?
I wonder if you miss what we had?
Or was that all on me?
Did I miss something?
Was I being played with like a yo-yo?
Why did I love you?

*I still do, and that's why this bugs the hell out of me.*
*Inside knowing I have these thoughts months later.*
*You left me as if I would be ok pretending like you*
*never existed.*
*Simply stripping me from every part of your life.*
*Sometimes it's the love I despise.*
*But it's the love that had me hooked.*

# Let It Be

*I feel incredibly dumb for saying this, but this is the transparent truth. I hope our paths cross again. I pray the universe brings our spirits together. I imagine our energies searching for each other.*

*I want to feel the laws of attraction pull us back together, even if it's our last conversation so deep that I can finally see the full scope and sequence of your choices and feelings.*

*Your mind is so beautiful even on the dark side of things. You captured my attention because under all the tears poured, traumas, and memories... there being illuminated was a beautiful love.*

*Love is the strength to know this isn't your permanent place in life. Love is knowing you experienced the best, yet was not ready to step up to the plate. Love is letting go of the woman of your dreams because your life is in chaos. Love is cutting all communication to keep that person from the toxicity invading your world. Love is being unresponsive to the person you love most because you have no answer that would make up for the heartbreak you caused.*

*But true, rich love is forgiveness.*
*Not to let go but to let it be.*
*That is true peace, and that is my true love.*
*It's just between you and me.*

# Rainbow Of Faith

To conquer this rock bottom that many fear is to face the reality of the situation. Own everything that made this moment what it was. Own everything holding your conscious back from moving forward.
Just admit it.
Reflect on it.
Talk about it.
Pray about it.
Trying to brush these critical elements under the mat will not work.
Pushing them far back in your mind is not an option. At this moment... getting OVER IT is not the answer.
This is the time to go through it.
Feel it all.
Remember it all.
It's in those small details where you will get a glimpse of who you were in those moments. That is the spark you need to remind yourself of all the beautiful things God put inside of you.
It's not what's on you, but more of what exudes from within.
No person, situation, or environment can take any of that away.

**Author Reflection:**
*I got here because I let those things cause me to lose faith. To get through this rock bottom, you have to believe that you can. One can never overcome difficulty with a half-*

*constructed mindset. You have to believe in the skills and talents God placed inside of you wholeheartedly. You have to believe in your strength to create a vision of hope to breakthrough.*

*You have to remember those dreams of using your gifts to make a difference.*

*You have to love those things that make you unique.*

*You have to own the reality of what's in front of you to get THROUGH IT.*

*The majority of the time, we choose to get over rather than through. It's the process of going through it that will bring strength, wisdom, and clarity. That is where the golden pot sits under your rainbow of fear, anxiety, and doubts—simply gracing the skies of hope exceptionally constructed in your mind.*

# Ownership

You are getting through it, and the healing process is ready to ignite a higher frequency of self-love.

# My Negatives

*I started this entry reasonably before I believed in my worth, value and could see the light at the end of my tunnel. I have had to rebuild my self-respect from the inside out. I had to realize I am nothing without my negatives, insecurities, and my past. Where I went wrong was limiting things that made me feel good on the outside for a temporary individuals whose comfort replaced my own.*
*But the way they made me feel.*
*The way they treated me.*
*The way they mended me into their world.*
*It's just simply the little things.*
*Just because our love story ended real raggedy... I have to take the good and the bad. Yin and Yang. Some would judge and say that you and I together was a significant negative from the outside looking in. I would say my negative is the way you ended things. The way you shut me out like a terrorist trying to break into the Fort Knox of your mind, your heart, and your soul.*
*All I wanted was to know WHY?*
*I wish it were just as easy for me as it was for you.*
*That was the difference I hadn't seen between us too.*
*Some people are raised in love, and some are raised in survival. You use the illusion of love as a means of self-preservation, not caring who it's given to.*
*I've learned.*

*I'll grow, and I hope one day I can thank you for this.*
*I'm nothing without my negatives, and you've been the*
*biggest one of them all.*
*THX*

# Elevated Taste

*All you gave me was a false taste of falling deeply in love. That moment we had felt so real. Unfortunately, I had to swallow the significant fact that it was just that... a moment. Admitting that I love you for the first time shook me to my core. By vocalizing that truth, positioned you to have the direct line of fire to kill my spirit. My heart was like a sitting duck waiting for you to pull the trigger. You achieved your goal and had your exit strategy locked and loaded. So quickly you found someone new. Not a replacement because no one can ever exude the essence of my energy, aura, and pure solitude.*
*It wasn't the someone new that hurt. It was the fact that the first time in my life, I stepped outside of my pride to fight for love.*
*My person.*
*My soulmate.*
*It was pointless.*
*You already checked out with the exchange overlapping.*
*To fill the void of my presence no longer being there.*
*The beauty of this... If I can feel like this*
*about your a\*\*, it will be so much more powerful when I find the person truly meant for me.*
*Someone available, someone who is spiritually connected.*

*Someone willing*
*to grow individually to support our collaboration.*
*Someone who will be patient.*
*someone that is ambitious.*
*Someone who is creative.*
*Someone who will stay faithful and committed.*
*Someone who trusts.*
*Someone I can trust.*
*Someone who will love me for me.*
*Someone who appreciates the big and little things.*
*Someone who spoils me.*
*Someone that makes me laugh.*
*Someone who likes to travel.*
*Someone who wants to engage and be hands on with their family.*
*Someone who likes to be of service to all mankind.*
*Someone who is passionate.*
*Someone willing to learn and understand different perspectives.*
*Someone who wants to include me in their life.*
*Someone who admires and respects me.*
*Someone I am inspired by and can respect.*
*Someone that makes me happy.*
*I have identified my worth and love for myself.*
*I know what I want.*
*I have elevated my taste.*

# Final Exam

Been asking for all the pieces to this broken masterpiece. Wanting to fill the gaps as if that would mend the floating pieces to your heart.
Many would ask, why do you care?
Would you even want to know the truth?
Well, when you are forced to rebuild your self-respect from the inside out, the most extraordinary assessment of that growth stems from how you handle the results. You spent months and conversations trying to rearrange this stupid stagnation. This repeating pattern of thoughts. Thoughts of the people who had hurt you and ultimately were true disappointments. Yet you are placing blame from many angles, including the person seen reflecting in your mirror.
Why are you in search of this ongoing why?
It's because you are in hopes of discovering an appropriate reason to fill that blank space that has remained empty for months.
With time ticking away, still concerned about why this was the outcome suited for you.
Time spent feeling everything.
Time spent growing and flowing.

Time spent forgiving through transparency.
Time spent gaining acceptance through reflection.
Time spent taking ownership.
Time spent being okay with not knowing what if.
It is in that particular moment; God will test you to see if your growth can stand the test of time. It is a test to see if you finally choose yourself. This will be the moment to apply the textbook of clarity you have been studying for months. What you do with this test will ultimately prove if that time spent studying was truly enough.
Times up; this is the final exam.

# Healing

You want to love again.
You will love again.
Standing side by side with that person creating something remarkable. Something magnificent.
Holding their hand as they gaze so passionately into your eyes. This someone new is compelled to acknowledge the value of your existence in this partnership.
The love they'll feel for you will be  perfectly manifested out of hope, prayer, and patience.
It's familiar.
As you once loved so freely.
Allow the transparency of your flowing feelings to be so vividly displayed in this moment...
no everlasting experience.
This someone new will love you so effortlessly. They will see that your radiant spirit demands to be loved. It demands to be appreciated. This love requires commitment as your heart shines with such a rare beauty finally being discovered, protected, and valued.
All that to say.
This is it.
This is what you've wanted, but something is holding you back from accepting it.
What could it be?
The acknowledgment will seemingly put the ownership of your desires in the palm of your hands. Your heart is still

healing from the luminous shards of pain that
penetrated so deep. Leaving fragmented
reminders of true loves pasts. These
fragments exist because you have allowed
them the space to dwell.
You have the power.
The power to choose what holds weight in
your heart.
The power to foster and maintain this
sickening bond.
It's up to you to let it be.
To love yourself so iridescently.

# Contract

*This was created to script out a contract in honor of myself and the elevation of faith I am nurturing with God. I have read this every day, slowly gaining undoubtable belief in the construction period God has placed me in. This was a way to forgive myself as a reminder of the light I dimmed within so overwhelmed with circumstances and temporary situations. I vocalize this daily as a reminder of the loss I went through to rebuild this more robust, confident, and faithful woman I see in the mirror. Some days I've read it and felt nothing. Some days I've read it, and it brought tears to my eyes. Some days I've read it, and I smiled. Some days I've read it, praying for better days to come. Some days I've read it, wondering when this grey area will be over. Someday I will not have to read it, as it will be a script embraced by my soul proving I made it.*

*I _____ vow to love honor and respect myself as well as God. I promise to live each day the way God has planned and to put faith in Him. I promise to communicate to gain clarity actively. I promise to move intentionally without a rush. I promise to think and live with integrity, knowing God has me covered. I promise to instill and plant this seed within others. I am strong. I am smart. I am talented. I am beautiful. I am kind. I am supportive. I am capable. I am blessed. I can do anything. I believe in myself and know God will guide me how he sees fit. I will no longer stress about the unknown or the things out of my control.*

*Signature: _____ Date:_____*

# Selfish

Choose to be selfish about your happiness through the transparency of your iridescent heart. The light at the end of the tunnel is so warm and radiant. The source of this light shines from within.

Remind yourself daily:

- You did not blow your blessing; it was just a lesson to learn.

- Do not allow a person, an environment, or situation to possess a power that overwhelms your spirit.

- You do not have to be perfect to flourish in the grey areas. You are deserving of grace and patience.

- Be transparent about how you feel, thus ignite the healing process.

# Iridescent Lingo

In this journey, a new lingo is only to be decoded through this book.

# Ir•ides•cent
/ˌirədes(ə)nt/   adjective

Exposing luminous true colors displayed from different perspectives. One's true colors are the emotions, thoughts, and memories that reside in their heart, waiting to be released through beautiful transparency.


# Ir•ides•cent Heal•ing
/ˌirədes(ə)nt/   /hēliNG/  noun

The process of using transparency to make one's heart, mind, and soul healthy again.

# Meet The Author

Salina Trahan
Born October 9, 1995, this lively libra sure knows how to balance it all. Salina Trahan grew up in the energetic city of Denver, Colorado. She is currently a passionate educator for Atlanta Public Schools. Her love to Educate Youth Everywhere led Salina Trahan to ignited her journey of promoting self-care to the world. Salina loves to create experiences exposing others to a variety of self-care practices. She hosted her first self-care conference on the campus of Clark Atlanta University in the spring of 2019. This excellent opportunity left students feeling more knowledgeable about self-care and how to apply practices to daily routines. Salina has a vested interest in discovering and expanding her awareness of different self-care practices to support mental health. She showcases her findings through her written blog on www.sincerelysalina.com and her YouTube podcast *Happy :Our*. Salina is also actively engaged with followers on Instagram and Facebook regularly posting motivating videos and information. Salina's goal is to help others learn to heal from the grey areas life can produce through beautiful Iridescent Healing.

www.ingramcontent.com/pod-product-compliance
Lightning Source LLC
Chambersburg PA
CBHW071419040426
42445CB00012BA/1222